I Can Tell by Touching

by Carolyn Otto

illustrated by Nadine Bernard Westcott

HarperCollins*Publishers*

The *Let's-Read-and-Find-Out Science* book series was originated by Dr. Franklyn M. Branley, Astronomer Emeritus and former Chairman of the American Museum–Hayden Planetarium, and was formerly co-edited by him and Dr. Roma Gans, Professor Emeritus of Childhood Education, Teachers College, Columbia University. Text and illustrations for each book in the series are checked for accuracy by an expert in the relevant field. For a complete catalog of Let's-Read-and-Find-Out Science books, write to HarperCollins Children's Books, 10 East 53rd Street, New York, NY 10022.

Let's Read-and-Find-Out Science is a registered trademark of HarperCollins Publishers.

Library of Congress Cataloging-in-Publication Data
Otto, Carolyn.
    I can tell by touching / by Carolyn Otto ; illustrated by Nadine Bernard Westcott.
        p.   cm. — (Let's-read-and-find-out science. Stage 1)
    Summary: Explains how the sense of touch helps to identify everyday objects and familiar surroundings.
    ISBN 0-06-023324-9. — ISBN 0-06-023325-7 (lib. bdg.) — ISBN 0-06-445125-9 (pbk.)
    1. Touch—Juvenile literature.   [1. Touch.   2. Senses and sensation.]   I. Westcott, Nadine Bernard, ill.
II. Title.   III. Series.
QP451.O88   1994   93-18630
152.1'82—dc20   CIP
                                                                                                           AC

1   2   3   4   5   6   7   8   9   10
❖
First Edition

The illustrations in this book were done with pen and ink, acrylic, and watercolor on Arches 100 pound cold press watercolor paper.

I Can Tell by **Touching**

I like to sit in our kitchen
and draw pictures with crayons.
When I close my eyes,
I still know where I am.
I can hear our refrigerator hum.
I smell the food we had for lunch.

I can tell I'm in the kitchen
because I hear and smell. But . . .
I know *exactly* where I am
only because I can feel.

I feel my back against the back of the chair,
and my seat on the hard chair seat.

I feel my elbows on the kitchen table.
The table is solid and smooth.
When I touch the table with my hands,
my fingers slide over the wood.

I can feel my drawing paper.
I feel five and a half fat crayons.

My hands tell me:
    the table is big and polished smooth,
    the paper is thin and flat,
    my crayons are fat and waxy.

I touch my picture of our bunny,
who lives in his own hutch.
The bunny in my picture is flat.
His crayon fur feels slick.
A real bunny feels rounder.
Real fur is warm and silky.
My hands can tell the difference.
My hands can tell by touching.

RABBIT
FOOD

My sister says it's time for our walk.
She wants me to leave the bunny alone.
She holds my hand very tightly.
She squeezes and pulls me along.
I can feel my feet in my socks,
and my socks slipping in my shoes.

Beneath my shoes something crunches,
something grinds and shifts around.

Even if I close my eyes,
I know we're on the gravel path.

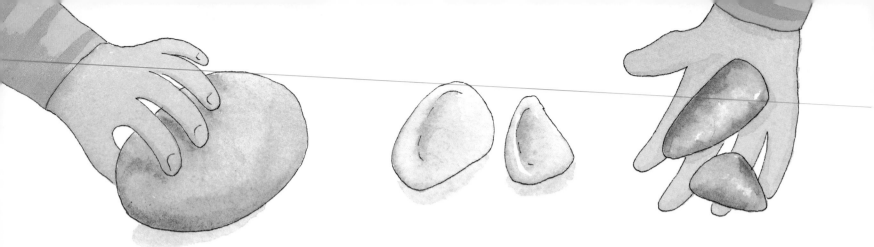

Rocks can feel like chicken eggs or seashells,
like arrowheads, potatoes, or just plain rocks.
Rocks can feel sandy or crumbly,
but most rocks feel hard.

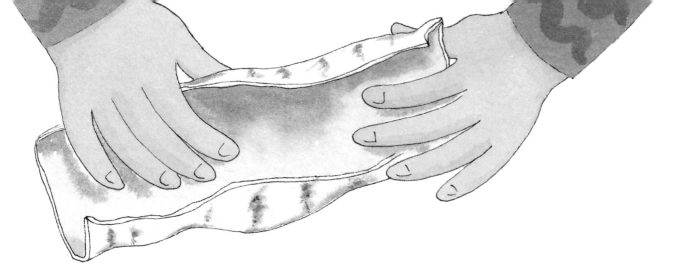

Some trees have bark that feels like paper.
The bark is thin and smooth.
A pine tree has bark that feels rough.
Pine needles are sharp and sticky with sap.

Under my feet grass feels like carpet,

but my fingers can feel each blade.
Grass feels warm in the sun and cool in the shade.

My hands tell me:
   the shape of a rock,
   whether bark is smooth or rough,
   the difference between carpet and grass.

I can tell where the sun has been,
and where the shade feels cool.
I can tell by touching.

I feel something brush my legs,
something fluffy, someone plump!
A puppy is soft on the outside,
wild and wiggly underneath.
A puppy's kiss is very wet.

This is the hill we slide down in winter.
We always roll down when it's warm.

I feel the hill bumping my shoulders.
I feel my shoes thumping the ground.
I feel myself rolling and rolling,

until I stop still at the end.

I feel the earth beneath me
and the hot sun overhead.

I feel grass and a dry dandelion
that's ready to fly into fluff.
I can tell by the way it feels.
I can tell by touching.

What can you tell by touching?

You can feel with your feet or legs,
your arms, your head, or your elbows.
Your skin is sensitive all over.
But you feel more with your hands.
Your hands will tell you the most.
You can find this out for yourself.
You'll need an orange, a tennis ball,
and a friend or your sister to help you.

Ask your friend to close her eyes.
Gently touch her knee with the orange.
Touch her shoulder or arm with the ball.
See if she can tell the difference
between a tennis ball and an orange.
Now put the orange in her hands.
Let her hold the tennis ball.
She'll know right away which is which.
Her hands will feel the difference.

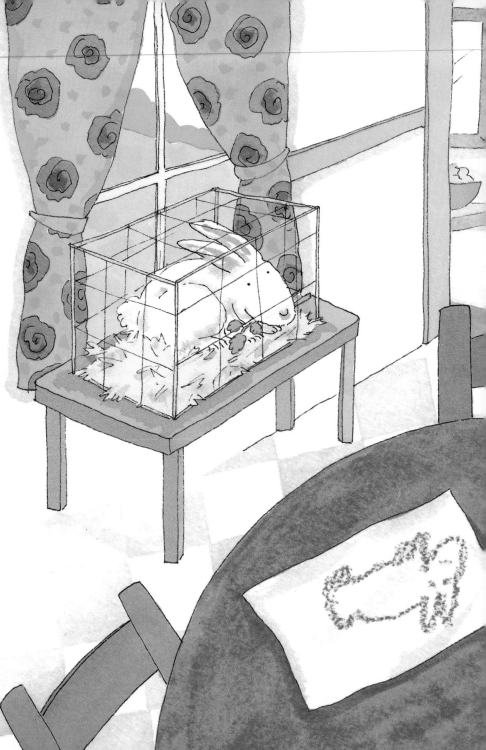

If you don't have an orange or a tennis ball,
you may use an apple, a potato, or a rock.
You can try this experiment with anything.
See what you can tell by touching.

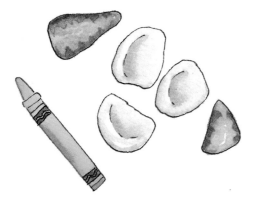